I AM

Published by ***Verse One Enterprises***
An Imprint of *E. Marcel Ministries*
www.emarceljones.com

ISBN: 9798439225842

Dedication

To all who contributed to the success of this writing project - **YOU ARE THE BEST!**

Shout out to all my FACERS on Facebook for your input and support; to K.D. (a musical genius) for your vision and musical collaboration; and to the Great I AM for Your inspiration and guidance.

"I AM what God says I AM —
Nothing more and nothing less."

Contents

Introduction

Congratulations! You have taken the first step towards improving your life.

Because our lives are surrounded by so much negativity, any positivity we encounter refreshes our soul. Racial insults are now common, but affirming words can heal years of pain. Body shaming frequently happens on most social media platforms. But, a word of affirmation can restore a person's self-esteem.

Perhaps the strongest, most heartfelt affirmation ever recorded was spoken by a Father to His Son. The affirmation is captured in the Holy Bible (Matthew 3:17), as God sends the most heavenly tone from heaven as His Son, Jesus, is being baptized in the Jordan River. "This is my son, in whom I am well pleased," God remarks (ESV). What a way to kick off your public ministry — by having your father place his signature directly on you in the presence of the world.

Our heavenly Father is still affirming us through His Word. His words are like a soothing balm to our soul, especially given the negativity many of us face daily.

We all will experience negative images, words, or actions at some point in our lifetime. This is precisely why <u>I AM</u> is so necessary for everyone to read. <u>I AM</u> is filled with strong affirmations that will encourage the mind, body, and soul.

Ironically, <u>I AM</u> was birthed out of a social media post. The post asked participants to complete the following statement: **I am** __________. During the days that followed, hundreds of people contributed their own personal affirmations. The response was so overwhelming that I decided to compile them all into one writing project. And, voila´, just like that, <u>I AM</u> was born.

I pray you will become stronger, bolder, and wiser as you journey through the pages that follow. I cannot wait to hear how God's affirmations have transformed your life.

Dr. E. Marcel Jones

PREACHER · TEACHER · LEADER

HOW TO USE:

Please note, the affirmations contained in **I AM** truly have transformative power. The contents of each page are designed to help readers push past the hindrances that prohibit their personal growth and realize the path towards their divine destiny. Affirmations are listed in alphabetical order and are divided into sections that contain four pages:

1. *The **Illustration** section (including an inspiring scripture and quotation)*
2. *The **Manifestation** section (reader engages in a thought-provoking prompts)*
3. *The **Prayer** section (provides an intimate opportunity to converse with God)*
4. *The **Reflection** section (which allows you to journal your thoughts freely)*

The best approach to reading this book is to meditate on a ***single*** affirmation each week. As you internalize the affirmation at the beginning of the week, set aside some time throughout the week to complete the remaining pages. Take your time and enjoy discovering all of the positive attributes that make you the incredible person you are. Remember, your story begins and ends with YOU!

I AM AMAZING

"You're amazing just the way you are." Bruno Mars

You are one amazing person. Do you realize the greatness that lies within your soul? You are amazing at what you do, how you think, what you speak, and who you are. You have creativity like none other and a style like no one else. And, even if others think of you as just mediocre or subaverage, you know that you are simply amazing. There's more of you waiting to be revealed. In fact, the world is awaiting your fullest potential. So, keep being the amazing individual you are and never dim your light to satisfy others who can't stand your shine!

I Corinthians 3:16
Do you not know that you are God's temple and that God's Spirit dwells in you?

What is something weighing heavily on your mind right now?

Prayer

Father, thank you for making me an amazing person. Every part of my being is amazingly created to worship you and accomplish amazing things. I'm blessed to know an amazing God.

I AM AMBITIOUS

"Keep away from those who try to belittle your ambitions. Small people always do that, but the really great make you believe that you too can become great." Mark Twain

You are ambitious and make no apologies for it. Because, your ambition is the hunger that drives you to reach your goals, achieve what others said could not be done, and arrive at the place you were destined to be. It's the ambition within you that provides you the stamina to endure and that same ambition that wakes you early the next morning to do it all over again. Ambition will open doors that your knowledge cannot and will take you further than your grit and grind can handle. Never lose your determination to succeed!

Colossians 3:23
Whatever you do, work heartily, as for the Lord and not for men

What are you looking forward to doing this week?

____

____

____

____

____

____

____

____

____

____

Prayer

Father, help me to maintain my ambitious spirit. I want to achieve great things in life and cannot do it without your power and will. To you be the glory for the things I've yet to achieve.

I AM ANCHORED

"Storms make tress take deeper roots." Dolly Parton

You are anchored and rooted in every area of your life. Your family roots run deep; your spiritual walk is firmly connected to God's Word. Your values, core relationships, and faith help anchor you and steady you, enabling you to withstand unsettling times. The more you've encountered, the deeper your roots have anchored in the soil around you. No wonder you're able to stand tall after the storms and challenges have battered your soul throughout life - because you kept your roots intact and remained loyal to your beliefs and convictions. Though the storms keep on raging in your life, your soul remains anchored in the Lord!

Psalm 62:6
Truly he is my rock and my salvation; he is my fortress, I will not be shaken.

Manifestation

What's causing you some concern, right now?

____

____

____

____

____

____

____

____

Prayer

Father, I thank you for keeping me anchored in your Word, your Will, and your Ways. Because you've grounded me, my life is steady and my spirit is at peace. I am assured that no storm in life is stronger than the anchor of your love for me.

I AM ANOINTED

"You are anointed. You are equipped. You are empowered. This is your season to reach new heights." Joel Osteen

There is an anointing on your life that enables you to accomplish the assignments over your life. You have the tools necessary to complete the tasks before you. You have been empowered to go the whole nine yards. Whatever you've been charged with or commissioned to do, you will achieve it. I know it gets cloudy at times and sometimes your faith might waiver, but those are just temporary distractors. You've got this — you will graduate; you will open that business; you will publish that book; you will be successful. Because, you've been anointed to win!

Psalm 23:5
You prepare a table before me in the presence of my enemies; you anoint my head with oil; my cup overflows.

Manifestation

Who are your accountability partners?

____

____

____

____

____

____

____

____

____

Prayer

Father, I can feel your anointing all over me. You are the one that gives me the power to stand, the power to succeed, the power to impact this world for your kingdom. You have anointed me to win in all that I do.

I AM AUTHENTIC

"We are constantly invited to be who we are." Henry David Thoreau

You are genuine and fully authentic. You are true to yourself and all that you will become. Even when it comes to others, you remain honest with them because you know no other way but to be authentic. Brother, you are the real deal! Sister, you are a 24-karat soul! Your authenticity began when you discovered who you truly were and made the decision to be that person every day, on purpose. When you refused the labels that others were attempting to attach to you, you started the journey towards being authentic. Congratulations on discovering who you are and revealing the person you are becoming.

Proverbs 27:19
As water reflects the face, so one's life reflects the heart.

What is something that you have had to overcome in life?

Prayer

Father, the more I take on the image of your Son, Jesus Christ, the more authentic I become. I don't want to be considered fake but want to be real and authentic. I don't want a fake religious experience but desire a real authentic relationship with you.

I AM BEAUTIFULLY CONSTRUCTED

"The first step to becoming what God made you to be is to stop worrying about what others want you to be." Rick Warren

You are beautifully constructed and a wonder to behold. God, himself, took the time to design, construct, and refine every detail of your anatomy and soul. Not even the Taj Mahal can match the architectural creativity and beauty you possess. What some might deem as a flaw or defect is merely a sign of the individual character of your temple. From the top of your head to the very soles of your feet, God's handiwork is to be appreciated and admired.

Genesis 2:7
Then the Lord God formed the man of dust from the ground and breathed into his nostrils the breath of life, and the man became a living creature.

Manifestation

What is the most beautiful part of your body and why?

____

____

____

____

____

____

Prayer

Father, thank you for the way you have constructed me. I'm in awe when I consider how frail I am outwardly but how strong I am inwardly. Every part of my body, you took the time to design and refine. You are the ultimate architect and sculptor — I'm blessed to have been clay in your hands.

I AM BLESSED

"When I started counting my blessings, my whole life turned around." Willie Nelson

You are blessed, my friend. In fact, when you consider all that you have encountered in life and the many obstacles that you have managed to overcome, you are a walking testimony of what a blessed life resembles. There are people who could not imagine surviving what you've endured. There are folks who would not believe all that God has brought you through. That's why today's affirmation is so befitting — because you've been given grace that lasts a lifetime.

Ephesians 1:3
Blessed be the God and Father of our Lord Jesus Christ, who has blessed us with every spiritual blessing in the heavenly places in Christ

Manifestation

What are you grateful for experiencing in life?

____

____

____

____

____

____

Prayer

Father, I am one blessed person! Just the fact that you saved me, sanctified me, redeemed me, justified me when I was at my worst is my greatest blessing. But, every day, when you awaken me, provide for me, guide me, inspire me, and protect me, you add to the blessings you've already given to me. Thank you for blessing me, God.

I AM BOLD

"It took me quite a long time to develop a voice, and now that I have it, I am not going to be silent."
Madeleine Albright

You possess a boldness deep within your heart that enables you to conquer things that seem improbable. There's an enriched level of confidence that is evident during tough times. In fact, you are not easily defeated because of the chutzpah and fearlessness you exhibit. When faced with an intimidating situation, you display the right amount of courage and nerve needed to overcome it. As you encounter various challenges in life, make certain your boldness remains unshakeable.

Deuteronomy 31:6
Be strong and courageous. Do not fear or be in dread of them, for it is the Lord your God who goes with you. He will not leave you or forsake you.

What is something that you've always wanted to do in life?

Prayer

Father, you have given me the boldness of a lion and the courage of one thousand soldiers. Now, please help me walk in this boldness that you have created within me. I need to be bold in my relationships, when making decisions, as I complete my tasks, and when ministering to the lost. By your power, I am BOLD!

I AM CALM

"In the madness, you have to find calm." Lupita Nyong'o

You are calm and filled with peace in your life. Even in the midst of tumultuous times, you have remained resolute in your calm, cool, and collected. Unlike many, you have not lost your mind over the trials of life. With all that life brings to agitate the human soul, your spirit has remained at peace. There are folks in your circle who depend on you to keep your head when they are losing theirs. You have the ability to look beyond stormy situations, see relief on the horizon, and declare, "It is well with my soul."

Isaiah 43:2
When you pass through the waters, I will be with you; and through the rivers, they shall not overwhelm you; when you walk through fire you shall not be burned, and the flame shall not consume you.

Manifestation

List all the things that relax you

____

____

____

____

____

____

____

Prayer

Father, whatever I face this week, help me to meet it with calmness and peace. I know the enemy loves to disrupt my life with distractions, but by your spirit, I can remain calm, cool, and collected. Thank you for giving me a restful spirit as I face unpredictable situations in life.

I AM CAPABLE

"I know I'm capable of greatness, and I'm expecting to reach that level." Aaron Rodgers

You are fully capable and competent! So, what are you waiting on? Why are you hesitating? You've got this! You've accomplished greater tasks than this before? Sure, this is new to you, but you must have forgotten that you're more than capable. God has invested too much in you for you not to be successful. So, roll up your sleeves, turn your big brain on, and let's get ready to do something great once again. No more doubting yourself or your abilities — it's time to WIN and WIN BIG1

Ephesians 6:10
Finally, be strong in the Lord and in the strength of his might

Manifestation

List some of the opportunities that have come your way this year.

Prayer

Father, this week will present many challenges. But, because you have blessed me with many abilities, I am capable of handling them all. Thank you for the gifts, talents, wisdom, and knowledge you have placed within me.

I AM CHOSEN

"God's business is adoption, Child. And, He has chosen you." Beth Moore

You have been chosen as a vessel and appointed the task of doing more than just existing. Your life is to be lived on purpose and with purpose. God selected you before you were even a thought. In fact, everything that has occurred in your life has been by His design. There's a reason why you have been on the path you're on now, a reason why the people in your life are still in your life and a reason why some were only seasonal. It's important for you to realize this but even more important to recognize WHO chose you. You were not the result of a popularity contest among family and friends, but you were hand-selected and divinely called by the God of all creation.

Romans 8:30

And those whom he predestined he also called, and those whom he called he also justified, and those whom he justified he also glorified.

Manifestation

Name three people that you are grateful for having in your life and tell why?

____

____

____

____

____

____

____

____

____

Prayer

Father, thank you for choosing me before the foundations of the world were laid. And, thank you for giving me purpose as one of your chosen vessels. Now, I pray that you strengthen me to represent your kingdom with integrity and honor. Because, I am chosen by the King.

I AM CONTENT

"I am content; that is a blessing greater than riches; and he to whom that is given need ask no more."
Henry Fielding

You are content and find satisfaction in every aspect of your life. You have finally arrived at the point in life where you recognize that material things can't produce a life of contentment. Your contentment is the result of finding fulfillment within. It is birthed out of a realization that your life has purpose and meaning. It is produced when you awaken with a great appreciation for the PRESENT. Even when you contribute to someone else's happiness, you discover even greater contentment in life.

Hebrews 13:5
Keep your life free from love of money, and be content with what you have, for he has said, "I will never leave you nor forsake you."

Manifestation

In your home, what are your grateful for owning?

____
____
____
____
____
____
____

Prayer

Father, I am content. Things are not perfect, but I am content. Things are evolving, but I remain content. I am not complacent, for fear that I would become comfortable. Nonetheless, you have made me content while I await every move you make on my behalf.

I AM ENOUGH

"I accept myself — that I am not on trial in my own eyes; that I value and respect myself." Nathaniel Branden

You are enough! Yes, you read this correctly - YOU ARE ENOUGH! There are people in your life who desire to change you and make improvements to you. I'm certain there are times you feel inadequate and know that you have some growing to do. But, despite what others demand from you or you demand of yourself, you are ENOUGH! What you give is ENOUGH. Who you are is ENOUGH. You are a valuable asset to your place of employment, to your family and friends, to your community, and to your church. You are already ENOUGH.

I Peter 2:9

But you are a chosen people, a royal priesthood, a holy nation, God's special possession, that you may declare the praises of him who called you out of darkness into his wonderful light.

Manifestation

If you had $1,000 to spend however you wanted to, what would you purchase and why?

____

____

____

____

____

Prayer

Father, I'm surrounded by a world of people who think I'm not enough. In their eyes, I fall short and am lacking in so many areas. But, you have assured me that I AM ENOUGH! There is nothing that is lacking because I am yours. There is nothing that I fall short of because you supply my every need. Thank you for making me MORE THAN ENOUGH.

I AM EVOLVING

"Everything on this earth is in a continuous state of evolving, refining, improving...You were not put on this earth to remain stagnant." Dr. Steve Maraboli

You can either choose to evolve or repeat what's already been done. If you're trying to move forward in life, you'll need to evolve. The world is evolving; people are you are evolving; nature is evolving. So, why not evolve as well? Evolving involves a shift from what you were to what you are becoming. The thought of shifting or transitioning from one version of yourself to another newer version of yourself can be downright scary and intimidating. But, those who resist their own personal evolution risk being left behind or dying.

Romans 5:2b - 4

And we boast in the hope of the glory of God. Not only so, but we also glory in our sufferings, because we know that suffering produces perseverance; perseverance, character; and character, hope.

Manifestation

Describe your life three years from now.

____

____

____

____

____

____

Prayer

Father, thank you for continuing to work on me in secret. Eyes have not beheld all that I will become. Ears have not heard all that you have in store for me. Daily, I am growing spiritually and evolving into the image of your Son, Jesus Christ.

I AM EXCELLENCE PERSONIFIED

"We are what we repeatedly do. Excellence, then, is not an act, but a habit." Aristotle

You are par excellence and everything you do is completed to the greatest quality. No, you're not perfect, but on your way to being perfected. Your life is a quest to be better, do better, achieve better, perform better, think better. And, it all begins with your attitude. Excellence isn't some skill that you pick up at a seminar or weekend retreat. But, excellence manifests when a person decides to pursue every area of their life (relationships, education, career, spirituality, etc.) with worth, aiming to make them all great!

Daniel 6:3

Then this Daniel became distinguished above all the other presidents and satraps, because an excellent spirit was in him. And the king planned to set him over the whole kingdom.

Manifestation

Describe three things you do really well.

Prayer

Father, you've raised the bar for my life and it is near perfection. I am obligated to walk in excellence, serve with excellence, and demand nothing short of excellence for my life. It's a high honor but one I know I can achieve each day by your power.

I AM FAVORED

"I'm still here; I'm still alive; I'm still blessed, on my way to my destiny, because the favor of God is on my life." Hezekiah Walker

You are favored! You're not lucky nor have you struck it rich. But, you are favored. You are the beneficiary of God's wealth. He makes everything you do prosper. Doors of opportunity open often. Each day you are gifted with countless options and opportunities, all designed to get you closer to God's ultimate plan for your life. When you're favored, health, wealth, and victorious living are soon to follow. And, grace and mercy follow you all the days of your life. No, you are not lucky...you are FAVORED!

Psalm 90:17
Let the favor of the Lord our God be upon us, and establish the work of our hands upon us; yes, establish the work of our hands!

Manifestation

What's something you keep putting off but need to do soon?

____

____

____

____

____

Prayer

Father, you have favored me! Thank you for favoring me with the right amount of sunshine for growth and just the right amount of rain for nourishment. You continually amaze me with your provisions. And, I cannot count the number of times you have favored me with open doors of opportunities. I owe you my life, for I am highly favored.

I AM FEARLESS

"You can never leave footprints that last if you are always walking on tiptoe." Leymah Gbowee

You are fearless, my friend! Some folks are intimidated by who's watching them. Others are hindered by those who sit on the sidelines mocking them. Still, many more never reach their goals because of the folks who attempt to block them. But, you acknowledge the power and strength to overcome that lies within you. Therefore, no one can stop you from being successful! Let those who hate you continue to watch you, mock you, and even attempt to block you. But, never allow their intimidation to abort the assignment you've been charged to complete.

Psalm 27:3
Though an army encamp against me, my heart shall not fear; though war arise against me, yet I will be confident.

Manifestation

What are you dreading this week?

Prayer

Father, you have not given me the spirt of fear. Instead, you have kept my mind in perfect peace and given me sound judgement. I am filled with holy boldness and stand bravely against the schemes of the enemy during his attacks. I do not fear evil because I know that, in you, I am victorious.

I AM FOCUSED

"Stay focused, go after your dreams, and keep moving toward your goals." L.L. Cool J

You are focused. You are so focused that you have managed to ignore the noise, the distractions, and the hype around you. Now, you are focused on the tasks at hand and focused on completing your assignments in life. And, you've got a lot to accomplish. I've seen your list! Just remember that when life becomes a little blurry, that's the time to adjust your focus. You will encounter obstacles, but keep your focus on the outcome, not the obstacles in your way. Don't look behind you or give attention to things beside you. But, keep your focus on what's ahead for you.

Matthew 6:33
But seek first his kingdom and his righteousness, and all these things will be given to you as well.

Manifestation

If your life was free from distractions this week, what is the one thing you would definitely accomplish?

____

____

____

____

____

____

Prayer

Father, you have helped me to maintain a focused life. But, this week, I'm asking you to help me not give attention to those distractions in my life. Regardless of what my opposition might be saying or doing to hinder me, I pray you will allow me to focus on your provision and the finish line.

I AM FORGIVEN

"We have been forgiven so much that nothing we forgive compares to the amount we have been forgiven."
Nicky Gumbel

You are forgiven. Now, go ahead and exhale. I know you have been waiting a long time to hear those words. But, despite what you said in the past, thought in the past, or did in the past, in Christ, you are forgiven. Have you repented from the transgressions you committed against others, against yourself, against God? If you have repented, the rest of the equation is up to God. And, the last time I checked God's Word, it still confirms that if you repent of your sins, God is faithful and just to forgive your sins and add an additional upgrade by cleansing you from all unrighteousness.

Psalm 103:12
As far as the east is from the west, so far has he removed our transgressions from us.

Manifestation

Have you forgiven yourself of everything that God has forgiven you for in life?______________ Why or Why not?

____

____

____

____

____

____

Prayer

Father, thank you for allowing the blood of your Son, Christ Jesus, to cleanse me and forgive me. My sins have been many, but you have forgiven me. I've fallen several times, but each time you forgave me. I am grateful for your forgiveness that sets me free.

I AM FREE

"May we think of freedom not as the right to do as we please, but as the opportunity to do what is right."
Peter Marshall

You are free! Your soul has been emancipated and your life has now been set free. You are no longer bound by the mistakes of your past - you are free. You are no longer condemned for the wrongs you were guilty of committing - you are free! Your freedom came at a cost but it was not a cost that you incurred. Your cost and all the penalties owed were erased when God's son went to the cross on your behalf. Thank God that you have been redeemed and set free. Now, live the rest of your life knowing that whom the Son has set free is FREE indeed.

Galatians 5:1
For freedom Christ has set us free; stand firm therefore, and do not submit again to a yoke of slavery.

Manifestation

What would you say to a friend feeling trapped by their past mistakes?

____
____
____
____
____
____

Prayer

Father, thank you for releasing me from the bondage of sin and making me free. Thank you for liberating me from the opinions of others so that I can walk confidently in my calling. You have freed me by paying a debt that you did not owe. And, I'm eternally grateful.

I AM GIFTED

"The gifted man bears his gifts into the world, not for his own benefit, but for the people among whom he is placed; for the gifts are not his, he himself is a gift to the community."
Henry Ford

You are gifted! And, because of the gift that God has placed within you, you are charged to find fulfillment by utilizing this gift to the benefit of others. You are not gifted for your own gain, but you are gifted to make the world around you better. You must always protect the gift within you. In fact, guard it against corruption and always exercise it with a sense of urgency. Never tuck away your gift for future use, but look for opportunities to use it daily.

James 1:17
Every good gift and every perfect gift is from above, coming down from the Father of lights with whom there is no variation or shadow due to change

Manifestation

How do you know that you are gifted?

____

____

____

____

____

____

Prayer

Father, I am discovering my gifts each day, and I endeavor to use them for your glory. If there are any gifts that remain dormant in my life, I pray that you will stir them up and awaken them in my spirit that I might maximize them for the kingdom. I am grateful for the gift and even more grateful for the Giver.

I AM GOD'S CHILD

"You are God's child, His creation - Destined for heaven and part of His family." Max Lucado

You are a child of God. Your earthly parents were responsible for birthing you, naming you, and nurturing you to adulthood. But, it was your heavenly father that knew you long before you were even conceived. God had a relationship with you long before your earthly parents even thought of you. Since your birth, God's love has continually sustained you, kept you, protected you, and provided for you. He is your Father and you are His child. And, nothing will ever separate you from His love.

Galatians 3:26
For in Christ Jesus you are all sons of God, through faith.

Manifestation

Name three benefits of being a child of God?

____

____

____

____

____

____

Prayer

Father, you are my creator, and I am your child. I love you and delight in calling you Daddy! I want to honor you and our relationship all the days of my life. Thank you for affirming me and adopting me as your child.

I AM GRATEFUL

"Always have an attitude of gratitude." Sterling K. Brown

You should be grateful for the blessings in your life. Every time you awaken gives you a reason to be grateful. The fact that you have people in your life that genuinely care about you is a reason to be grateful. The things you have survived and the dangers that didn't take your life should give you cause to express gratitude. While some are grateful for having food to eat, someone else is grateful for just having an appetite. Having a bed to rest your head is considered a blessing, but a bed cannot guarantee you'll sleep through the night. There are countless reasons to express gratitude if you open your eyes to the blessings around you.

Lamentations 3:22-24

The steadfast love of the Lord never ceases; his mercies never come to an end; they are new every morning; great is your faithfulness. "The Lord is my portion," says my soul, "therefore I will hope in him."

Manifestation

Recall three happy moments that occured during your childhood?

____

____

____

____

____

____

Prayer

Father, I refuse to wait until Thanksgiving Day to express my gratitude towards you. I'm grateful for caring for me, for keeping your eyes on me, and for the plans you have for me. The gratitude in my heart is the result of your love for me. Thank you!

I AM HAPPY

"Be happy with what you have. Be excited about what you want."
Alan Cohen

You are happy, and this is like medicine to your bones. Happiness leads to a lifetime of wellness. So, it's imperative that you maintain your happiness — it will bring wellness and wholeness to you and your household. Your place of employment will benefit from you being happy. Your social circle will be enriched by your happiness. And, your body will thank you for the happiness you experience. Your stress levels will decrease; blood pressure will return to normal levels; your heart rate will be regulated — all because you intentionally pursue happiness.

Proverbs 17:22
A cheerful heart is good medicine,
but a crushed spirit dries up the bones.

Manifestation

When you're at your happiest moment in life, it's usually because...

____

____

____

____

____

____

Prayer

Father, I am happy with my life. It took me a while to find this level of satisfaction with my career, my relationships, and myself. When I realized that things could be worse than they are right now, I started focusing on 99 other reasons to smile. And, as a result, I remain happy with my life.

I AM HEALED

"Healing is not an overnight process; it is a daily cleansing of pain, a daily healing of your life."
Leon Brown

Healing is a process that all of us will experience in life. It might be a scraped knee or a bruised heart. At some point, we all seek to be healed. Just know that healing doesn't mean that the wounds are no longer visible. Instead, it's when the wound no longer aches that you'll know you've been healed. When the wound doesn't prevent you from moving forward, you've been healed. The scars might still be present, though they fade with time. But, even with visible scars, you can still experience healing.

Isaiah 53:5
But he was wounded for our transgressions; he was crushed for our iniquities; upon him was the chastisement that brought us peace, and with his stripes we are healed.

What inspires you to be great?

____

____

____

____

____

____

Prayer

Father, thank you for healing me. Thank you that my heart has been healed from past hurts; my mind has been healed from past mistakes; my life has been healed from past disappointments, and my body has been healed from all diseases. I am healed because of your stripes, God.

I AM HOLY

"A holy life will produce the deepest impression." Dwight L. Moody

You are holy and have been made righteous by a holy God. Despite your sins of the past, God has declared you holy through Christ Jesus. And, because of the calling God has placed on your life, you must maintain a lifestyle of holiness. Maintaining a pure lifestyle is a daunting task but possible through the power of God's Spirit. Holiness is not an event or one-time action, but a lifestyle that every believer must strive to incorporate into their daily walk. Our thoughts must be holy; our ways must be holy; even our words must be holy.

I Peter 1:15-16
But as he who called you is holy, you also be holy in all your conduct, since it is written, "You shall be holy, for I am holy."

If you could eliminate three nasty habits, what would they be?

Prayer

Father, help me to remain holy. I desire to remain pure and undefiled. I pray that my thoughts remain holy and my ways remain holy. Sanctify my hands and hearts and let the words I speak be holy throughout today and always.

I AM INTELLIGENT

"Intelligence is not the ability to store information, but to know where to find it." Albert Einstein

We all possess a measure of intelligence. Some may be considered borderline genius while others might be classified as having a normal intelligence quotient (I.Q.). Regardless to the amount of intelligence you possess, however, how you use your intelligence is important to God. God has given you intelligence and His Spirit so that you can discern right from wrong or good from evil. With your intelligence, you have the ability to make sound decisions that will benefit you and your family. Thank God you are an intelligent child of God.

Proverbs 18:15
The heart of the discerning acquires knowledge, for the ears of the wise seek it out

Manifestation

hat was your best subject in school and why?

____

____

____

____

____

____

Prayer

Father, I realize that there are people who are smarter than I am, but I thank you for the level of intelligence that you have blessed me to possess. I am amazed that I comprehend even the most complicated matters and that what I don't understand, your spirit helps me to discern.

I AM KEPT

"I didn't always stick with God, but He always stuck with me." Denzel Washington

You are kept by the power of God. He has his eyes on you throughout the day. His hand is upon your every move. You are in his plan and He keeps your soul from being corrupted. Every time you walk out of your home, God keeps you from the dangers that lurk around you - those dangers that are seen and those that are unseen. What a mighty God you serve; that He thinks enough of you that He will not let your foot slip. Instead, he keeps you from falling and presents you faultless before the presence of His glory with exceeding joy.

Numbers 6:24-26
"'The Lord bless you and keep you; the Lord make his face shine on you and be gracious to you; the Lord turn his face toward you and give you peace.'"

Manifestation

In what ways has God been especially kind to you?

____

____

____

____

____

____

Prayer

Father, thank you for keeping me and caring for me. You are the lover of my soul and I adore you with all my heart, mind, and soul I only have to ask and you fulfill the desires of my heart. All the glory in my life belongs to you.

I AM LIMITLESS

"There is no limit to what our limitless God will do in response to a limitless faith." Smith Wigglesworth

You are limitless, my friend. Everything that could hinder you or prevent you from succeeding has no power over you. The barriers to your success have been removed because God has ordered your steps and your life is in His perfect will. There are no limits to what you can accomplish for the Kingdom of God or even in your personal life. Starting today, change your mindset from "I cannot because..." to "I CAN because..." Take the limits off your mind, body, and soul, and accomplish great things for Christ.

2 Timothy 1:7
For God gave us a spirit not of fear but of power and love and self-control.

Manifestation

What excuses have you used in the past that have prevented you from reaching your goals?

____

____

____

____

____

____

Prayer

Father, there is no limit to what you can do. And, because I belong to you, I too am limitless. I have an unlimited supply of resources, mercy, grace, and favor available at my request. I am not restricted or hindered because there are no limits to what I can become or do.

I AM LOVED

"To love someone is to see a miracle invisible to others."
Francois Mauriac

You are loved, my friend. No matter how many people have neglected you, failed you, forgotten you, or abused you — you are loved! You may not be loved by most people, but you are loved by the only one that counts - God! And, God's love for you will never fail. He promises that He won't ever leave you or forsake you. In fact, God's love is permanent and nothing will ever separate you from His love. God proved his love for you in that while you were still dead in your sins, God sent his Son Christ Jesus to die on your behalf. That's love!

Jeremiah 31:3
The Lord appeared to us in the past, saying:
"I have loved you with an everlasting love;
I have drawn you with unfailing kindness.

Manifestation

List the top three persons in your life that love you the most?

____

____

____

____

____

____

Prayer

Father, thank you for loving me when I was unlovable. You loved me in spite of my wretchedness and filthy soul. You loved me when I was at my worst and gave me your best to save me from hell. I feel your love and your presence even now and love you in return because you first loved me.

I AM MOTIVATED

"Don't judge each day by the harvest you reap but by the seeds that you plant."
Robert Louis Stevenson

Whatever got you up and running this morning is your motivator. Whatever fuels your passion and drive to live is your motivation. You, my friend, are motivated! And, the motivation you possess can propel you to higher heights and beyond a life of complacency. You are motivated to become a better and bolder person. You are well on your way to achieving great things. Don't allow the distractions in life to deter or discourage you. But, stay the course and remain motivated until the end.

Romans 15:13
May the God of hope fill you with all joy and peace as you trust in him, so that you may overflow with hope by the power of the Holy Spirit.

List three self-goals to achieve by the end of the year (one for your mind, one for your body, and one for your soul)?

Prayer

Father, I am motivated to accomplish all that you have assigned me to conquer today. I am excited to serve you and cannot wait to see what blessings you have in store for me throughout the day. Please shield me from any discouraging words or news and keep me enthusiastic about life.

I AM POWERFUL

"Never underestimate the power of dreams and the influence of the human spirit." Wilma Rudolph

You are filled with power! Within you lies the power to accomplish great feats, to both survive and succeed against all odds, to determine the path for your life, and even the power to press through any obstacles in your way. You are powerful! No, you're not some comic book superhero endowed with powers from a meteor shower, but you are God's creation, blessed with supernatural power that conquers the enemy. In fact, you are not just your average conqueror, but you are a "More Than" conqueror through Christ that strengthens you.

Philippians 4:13
I can do all this through him who gives me strength.

Which is stronger (your mind, body, or soul) and why?

Prayer

Father, you have given me the strength and power to overcome every weakness in my life. I am strong and when I am weak, then you are my STRENGTH. Help me not weaken throughout the day but remain strong in you, Lord. My strength depends on you.

I AM PROGRESSING

"If there is no struggle, there is no progress." Frederick Douglas

You have made huge strides since this time last year. Can't you see the differences in your life? You've been steadily progressing and improving. Sure, you've had a few setbacks from time to time, but when you compare where you are now to where you've come from, you have to admit that the Lord has brought you a mighty long way. Don't focus on what's happened in the past — forget those things. Instead, focus your eyes on the prize that lies ahead and keep progressing and pushing towards those goals.

Philippians 3:13-14
Brothers and sisters, I do not consider myself yet to have taken hold of it. But one thing I do: Forgetting what is behind and straining toward what is ahead, 14 I press on toward the goal to win the prize for which God has called me heavenward in Christ Jesus.

What's one thing you always take for granted and why?

____

____

____

____

____

____

Prayer

Father, you have helped me through many storms and to overcome many obstacles. You've been with me during my life's journey from the beginning, and I see your hand in every step I take. Because of you, I am progressing through this life and winning. Thank you that I am not the same person I used to be.

I AM PROSPEROUS

"Mediocrity is the worst enemy of prosperity." Henry Ford

Your life is prospering, my friend. Things are beginning to turn around in your favor and you're finally on your way to becoming the person God intends you to be. The plans you've had for your career, your relationships, your personal health are transpiring. God desires you to prosper and be in health, even as your soul prospers. That means that God is concerned about every aspect of what makes you - YOU. Enjoy the plans of prosperity that God has for you and watch how wonderful your future will be.

Jeremiah 29:11
For I know the plans I have for you," declares the Lord, "plans to prosper you and not to harm you, plans to give you hope and a future.

Where would be the most ideal place for you to live and why?

Prayer

Father, thank you for making my ways prosperous. I have not received everything I desire, but you have made sure I have not lacked in the things I need. You've given me an overflow of blessings, and I'm grateful for prospering and being in health.

I AM REDEEMED

"Without the redeeming power of Christ, we cannot halt our own moral slide." Charles Swindoll

You were once dead in your trespasses. But, now you have been made alive in Christ because you have been redeemed. It took the blood of one willing to sacrifice his life to save yours. And, because of this selfless act, your life is no longer your own. Your life belongs to Christ. What a joy it is to experience redemption, restoration, and renewal at the hands of a loving God. You don't have to carry around the weight of guilt or fear condemnation any longer because you have been redeemed!

I Corinthians 6:20
You were bought at a price. Therefore honor God with your bodies.

How do you spend time with family?

____

____

____

____

____

____

Prayer

Father, thank you for the purchase you made on the cross when Jesus sacrificed his life for mine. You have redeemed me and adopted me into your family. And, now, because of your redemptive power, I have been restored, and renewed as your child. I belong to You!

I AM RESILIENT

"Today, our very survival depends on our ability to stay awake, to adjust to new ideas, to remain vigilant, and to face the challenge of change."
Dr. Martin Luther King

Nothing can hold you down long because you are resilient. You've had your share of challenges, failures, and mistakes in life. But, none of them were able to defeat the purpose that lies within you. You are destined to live out God's plan. So, every time you're knocked around, you remain in the fight. And, every time you're knocked down and stepped on, you bounce back. You have this toughness in you that will not allow you to stay down, which is why you always seem to recover from every fall.

Habakkuk 2:3
For the revelation awaits an appointed time; it speaks of the end and will not prove false. Though it linger, wait for it; it will certainly come and will not delay.

Manifestation

What gives you strength to tackle each day?

____

____

____

____

____

____

Prayer

Father, you have given me resilience. Nothing can keep me down or take me out of the game of life because every time I'm knocked down, you strengthen me to get back up and try again. Help me to survive every storm, every attack and to keep going despite the obstacles I encounter.

I AM SAVED

"A drowning man cannot be saved until he is utterly exhausted and ceases to make the slightest effort to save himself." Watchman Nee

Salvation is at work in you right now. Because you're saved, you have been cleansed from your sins and made righteous before a perfect God. This means that you have been justified or your relationship with God has been repaired. Because your salvation is more about relationship than religion, you have access to God at all times. All of this is good news, but the greatest news is that we have eternal life to look forward to instead of eternal death in hell to await. Our salvation is secured by grace through our faith.

Acts 4:12
"Salvation is found in no one else, for there is no other name under heaven given to mankind by which we must be saved."

Describe your relationship with God?

Prayer

Father, thank you for salvation! You have saved me and promised me eternal life. My life is full of abundant blessings because you saved me. Thank you for not giving up on me when sin gripped my soul Thank you for the salvation I found by grace through faith.

I AM TALENTED

"I believe that every person is born with talent." Maya Angelou

There is no need for you to ever feel slighted or ashamed. Because, within you there are abilities that enable you to perform tasks, develop concepts, express ideas, and innovate life. You are talented. Some of your talents have been put to use throughout your life without you knowing what they were. Maybe you thought of it as something that felt natural and came with ease. But, it was actually your talent at work. If you search deep enough, you might even discover talents that have been dormant all your life, waiting to awaken and be put to use.

Ephesians 4:12
"Christ gave these gifts to prepare God's holy people for the work of serving, to make the body of Christ stronger."

Manifestation

If you were to perform before the King of a great nation, what talent would you display for him?

____

____

____

____

____

____

Prayer

Father, it has taken years for me to discover how talented I really am. Now that I recognize my God-given abilities, I can hardly wait to show the world what I have to offer! Help me protect my talents, develop my talents, and perfect my talents daily.

I AM THANKFUL

"Sometimes we need to remind ourselves that thankfulness is indeed a virtue." William Bennett

Have you ever taken the time to reflect on how fortunate you are to have life and come to the realization that you are one extremely blessed individual? Start counting from your earlier days as a child and keep adding up the number of things that you should be thankful for and I guarantee you'll run out of ink and paper before you exhaust the number of reasons you should be thankful. And, if you ever reach a point when you run out of reasons, take a second to inhale and then exhale and you'll discover yet another reason to be thankful.

Colossians 3:15
Let the peace of Christ rule in your hearts, since as members of one body you were called to peace. And be thankful.

The one thing that I'm thankful for right now is... Why?

____

____

____

____

____

____

Prayer

Father, I have so much to be thankful for right now. I'm grateful for my relationship with you, for the love of family and friends, the ability to make sound decisions, your protection and provision, for the health I enjoy and peace of mind you give to me each day. Thank you, Lord!

I AM THRIVING

"My mission in life is not merely to survive, but to thrive; and to do so with some passion, some compassion, some humor, and some style." Maya Angelou

To thrive literally means to prosper. It means you've decided that a life of mediocrity won't cut it. Thriving is a greater move than just striving or surviving. There are some that are content with living a substandard life. In fact, you don't have to look far to find folks who would rather accept what life has to offer (even if it's hardly anything) than to put forth the energy and drive it takes to grow beyond where they are right now. I know you want more out of life, out of your relationships, out of your career. As you strive, you'll find that you will thrive.

Psalm 1:1-3

Blessed is the man who walks not in the counsel of the wicked, nor stands in the way of sinners, nor sits in the seat of scoffers; but his delight is in the law of the Lord, and on his law he meditates day and night. He is like a tree planted by streams of water that yields its fruit in its season, and its leaf does not wither. In all that he does, he prospers.

You are most energized in the morning, afternoon, or evening?________________________
Why do you think this is so?

____

____

____

____

____

____

Prayer

Father, you help me every day to thrive and survive. No matter what circumstances I face or challenges I encounter, you empower me to press through them all and thrive anyhow. I'm amazed at how much I can accomplish each day, but I recognize it's only possible because of You!

I AM UNIQUE

"Be a voice, not an echo."
Unknown

The fact that there has never been and will never be an individual exactly like you is simply awesome! Sure, there's always the chance that you'll meet your celebrity twin or be mistaken by a stranger as someone they grew up with. But the truth of the matter is that you are unique! And, because of your uniqueness, you have the opportunity to impact this world like no one else. The world is waiting on your uniqueness to debut! We need your fresh outlook, your innovative viewpoint, your unique take on life. Don't bother copying anyone else. Delight in being uniquely YOU!

Psalm 139:14
I praise you, for I am fearfully and wonderfully made. Wonderful are your works; my soul knows it very well.

Manifestation

The most unique thing about you is...

____

____

____

____

____

____

Prayer

Father, I am uniquely designed. There is no one quite like me. Thank you for taking your time when creating me. I line and embrace who I am, who I am becoming, and who I will be! Some might call me different, but I know your touch made me unique.

I AM VICTORIOUS

"Acknowledge all of your small victories. They will eventually add up to something great." Kara Goucher

Who doesn't want to win in life? When you 're able to accomplish your goals and realize your dreams, those are victories. When you defy the odds and come out on top, that's a victory. When you resist doing the wrong thing and end up doing the right thing, that's a victory. Each day provides you with several opportunities to be victorious. In fact, just the fact that you awakened this morning is a victory worth celebrating. Be aware of the challenges ahead but never take your eyes off the victory that awaits you at the end of each day. You are victorious!

I John 5:4
For everyone who has been born of God overcomes the world. And this is the victory that has overcome the world—our faith.

What have you had to overcome during your adulthood?

Prayer

Father, Victory is mine. Victory is mine today. The world knows this. The enemy hates this. The victory on the cross gives me direct access to victory in life as well. You came that we might be victorious in you. Thank you, in advance, for every victory this week!

I AM VIGILANT

"Just 'cause you got the monkey off your back doesn't mean the circus has left town." George Carlin

Never let your guards down in life. But, always remain vigilant and watchful. Because, there's an enemy on the prowl that desires to destroy you. And, this enemy will use anyone and anything available to accomplish his agenda. This is why it's necessary for you to always be on the lookout for those with ulterior motives. Unfortunately, not everyone can be trusted. So, to protect your life, you must stay alert, remain sober and awake, and approach every situation with caution. Throughout each day, remain vigilant.

I Peter 5:8
Be sober-minded; be watchful. Your adversary the devil prowls around like a roaring lion, seeking someone to devour.

Manifestation

In what areas of your life could you be better organized?

____

____

____

____

____

____

Prayer

Father, you desire me to remain sober at all times. Because the enemy is on the prowl, you have made me a vigilant soldier. Help me to keep my hand to the plow and ever-watchful for the schemes of the enemy. By your power, I will remain alert and prepared.

I AM WHOLE

"Seek to be whole, not perfect."
Oprah Winfrey

Lord knows you've had your share of failures in life. But, the good news is that no matter how many faults you possess or how many failures you've experienced, in Christ, you are still WHOLE. Despite the phases of life you experience, you remain whole and complete. You've likely survived traumatic events that would have left the average person in pieces. But, not you! You remind me of our moon that displays different shapes depending on which phase it is in. Whether it's in quarter, half, or full phase, the moon is never fragmented but always whole. No matter how people view your circumstances in life, remember you are always complete - always whole in Christ.

I Thessalonians 5:23
Now may the God of peace himself sanctify you completely, and may your whole spirit and soul and body be kept blameless at the coming of our Lord Jesus Christ.

If you were an egg that had been cracked what pieces would be necessary for putting you together again?

Prayer

Father, there is no part of me that is not complete. I have been made whole because of the blood of Jesus Christ. I am not 1/2 of a person. I do not have 3/4 of what I need to be successful. But, I am completely and unapologetically whole.

I AM A WINNER

"Winners are not people who never fail but people who never quit."
Edwin Louis Cole

Every win in your life was the result of your decision to not quit. To win in life, you must continue to push past the obstacles, the naysayers, the haters, the failures and falls, and continue the race. Sometimes, just finishing is considered a WIN. Don't confuse your place in the race with your victory. This life is about surviving against all odds and finishing strong. There's a winner in you waiting to cross the finish line daily. Daily victories lie ahead for those who stay in the race.

2 Corinthians 2:14
But thanks be to God, who always leads us in triumph in Christ, and manifests through us the sweet aroma of the knowledge of Him in every place.

Celebrate three wins you've already experienced this year.

Prayer

Father, I am a winner because you have defeated the enemy. I don't ever have to settle for 2nd place or drop out of the race because you have already won the battles before I even begin the fight. I win and cannot lose because I am a conqueror in Christ. Help me run my race with patience and the promise of knowing that I win!

I AM WORTHY

"I am worthy of so much more than what I started to settle for."
Unknown

Despite others' opinions of you, you are worthy! Despite your past, you are worthy! Despite your own personal self-assessment, you remain worthy! Your value and worth is not determined by the calculations performed by people — their math is off! Your worth is predicated upon the deposits that God has made in your life. Within you is a soul that is far more valuable than the costliest gem. Your soul and the many gifts and talents you possess add worth to your life. Never discount your worth or contributions but remind yourself daily that you are worthy!

Matthew 6:26
Look at the birds of the air: they neither sow nor reap nor gather into barns, and yet your heavenly Father feeds them. Are you not of more value than they?

Manifestation

Is your life of No value, Some value, or High value?____________________ Why?

____

____

____

____

____

____

Prayer

Father, thank you for counting me worthy of your love. Because you created me, you also gave me worth. I'm no longer obligated to accept the labels and price tag others place on my life. But I am free to live a life that's worthy because of your Grace.

JUST AS I AM - by Charlotte Elliott (1835)

Just as I am - without one plea,
But that Thy blood was shed for me,
And that Thou bidst me come to Thee,
-O Lamb of God, I come!

Just as I am - and waiting not
To rid my soul of one dark blot,
To Thee, whose blood can cleanse each spot,
-O Lamb of God, I come!

Just as I am - though toss'd about
With many a conflict, many a doubt,
Fightings and fears within, without,
-O Lamb of God, I come!

Just as I am - poor, wretched, blind;
Sight, riches, healing of the mind,
Yea, all I need, in Thee to find,
-O Lamb of God, I come!

Just as I am - Thou wilt receive,
Wilt welcome, pardon, cleanse, relieve;
Because Thy promise I believe,
-O Lamb of God, I come!

Just as I am - Thy love unknown
Has broken every barrier down;
Now to be Thine, yea, Thine alone,
-O Lamb of God, I come!

Just as I am - of that free love
The breadth, length, depth, and height to prove,
Here for a season, then above,
-O Lamb of God, I come

Books By E. Marcel

Be sure to check out the following books available on Amazon

Life After High School Graduation
Life After College Graduation
Life After Divorce
Life After Loss

The Naked Truth:
The Gospel According to Singles
El Evangelio Según Los Solteros

Drop and Give God Ten
Suelta y Dale Diez a Dios

In Times Like These
En Tiempos Como Estos

The Best Sermon Note Taker For Men
The Perfect Sermon Note Taker for Women
The Sermon Note Taker for Busy Bodies

Dr. E. Marcel Jones serves as the Pastor of Cummings Street Church in Memphis, TN. He has published over a dozen inspirational books. For more information, visit www.emarceljones.com

Made in the USA
Coppell, TX
28 March 2022